TRANSFER QUEEN

Before you start to read this book, take this moment to think about making a donation to punctum books, an independent non-profit press,

@ https://punctumbooks.com/support/

If you're reading the e-book, you can click on the image below to go directly to our donations site. Any amount, no matter the size, is appreciated and will help us to keep our ship of fools afloat. Contributions from dedicated readers will also help us to keep our commons open and to cultivate new work that can't find a welcoming port elsewhere. Our adventure is not possible without your support.
Vive la open-access.

Fig. 1. Hieronymus Bosch, *Ship of Fools* (1490–1500)

TRANSFER QUEEN (MALE FIGURE DRAWINGS FROM THE NYC SUBWAY). Copyright © 2018 by A.W. Strouse and Patty Barth. This work carries a Creative Commons BY-NC-SA 4.0 International license, which means that you are free to copy and redistribute the material in any medium or format, and you may also remix, transform and build upon the material, as long as you clearly attribute the work to the authors (but not in a way that suggests the authors or punctum books endorses you and your work), you do not use this work for commercial gain in any form whatsoever, and that for any remixing and transformation, you distribute your rebuild under the same license. http://creativecommons.org/licenses/by-nc-sa/4.0/

First published in 2018 by punctum books, Earth, Milky Way.
https://punctumbooks.com

ISBN-13: 978-1-947447-63-9 (print)
ISBN-13: 978-1-947447-64-6 (ePDF)

LCCN: 2018945512
Library of Congress Cataloging Data is available from the Library of Congress

Book design: Vincent W.J. van Gerven Oei
Cover illustrations: Petty Barth

HIC SVNT MONSTRA

A.W. Strouse

with drawings by
Patty Barth

I'm obsessed with taking public transportation. I read about a guy in L.A. who rides the buses just to pick up people. A 'transfer queen'?

— John Waters

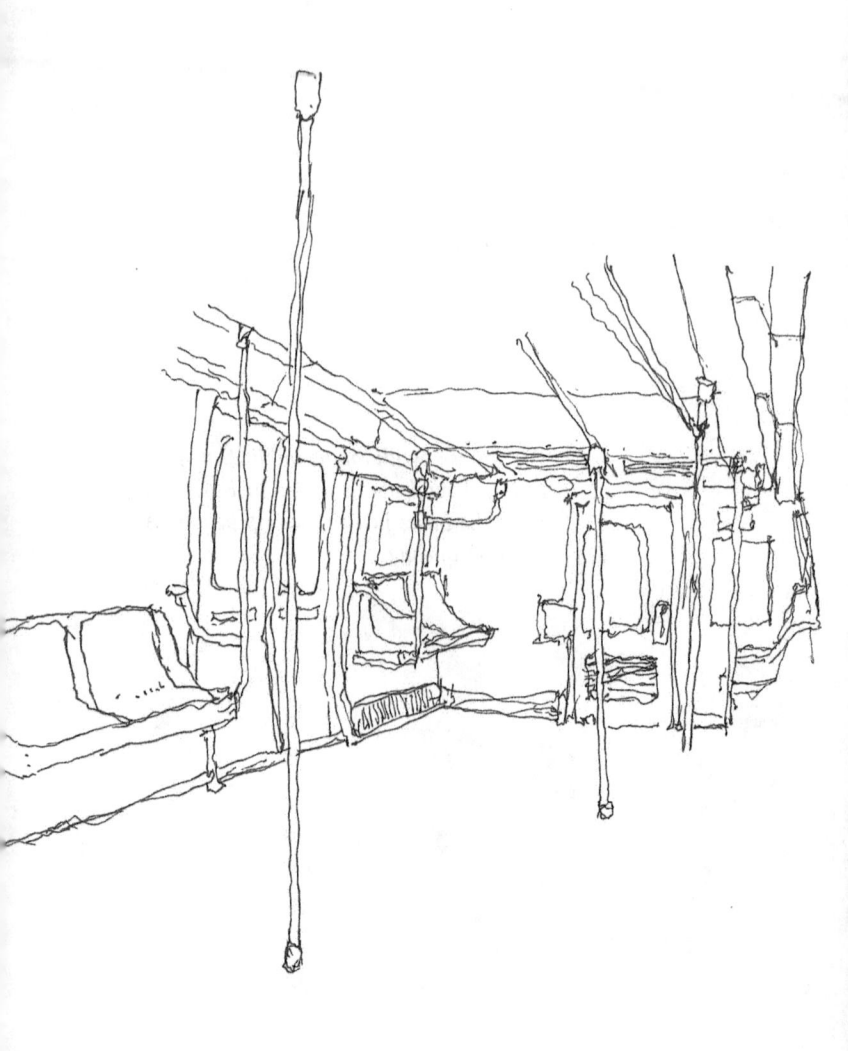

although i can tell
(with his hand
down his trousers)
that he is scratching
his butthole,
my muse will not
believe me

bearded men who trim their necks high
(this gym rat,
for example)
i file under
"botched circumcisions"

construction worker crosses his legs
leaning against the pole
his fat ass
way passed due

as this guy picks a molar
his attempt at secrecy
prolongs the dive

awakening from
an 8-stop nap
he immediately fellates
a NUTRAGRAIN bar

jailbait in a v-neck
bats his eyes
but i aint going down
that-a-way

muslim boy in a skirt
beside an older brother
wears only one glove

that dandy in the
polka-dot fedora
sports a non-foppish tote
from any old
DUANE READE

whatever he mumbles
causes his girlfriend
to scream

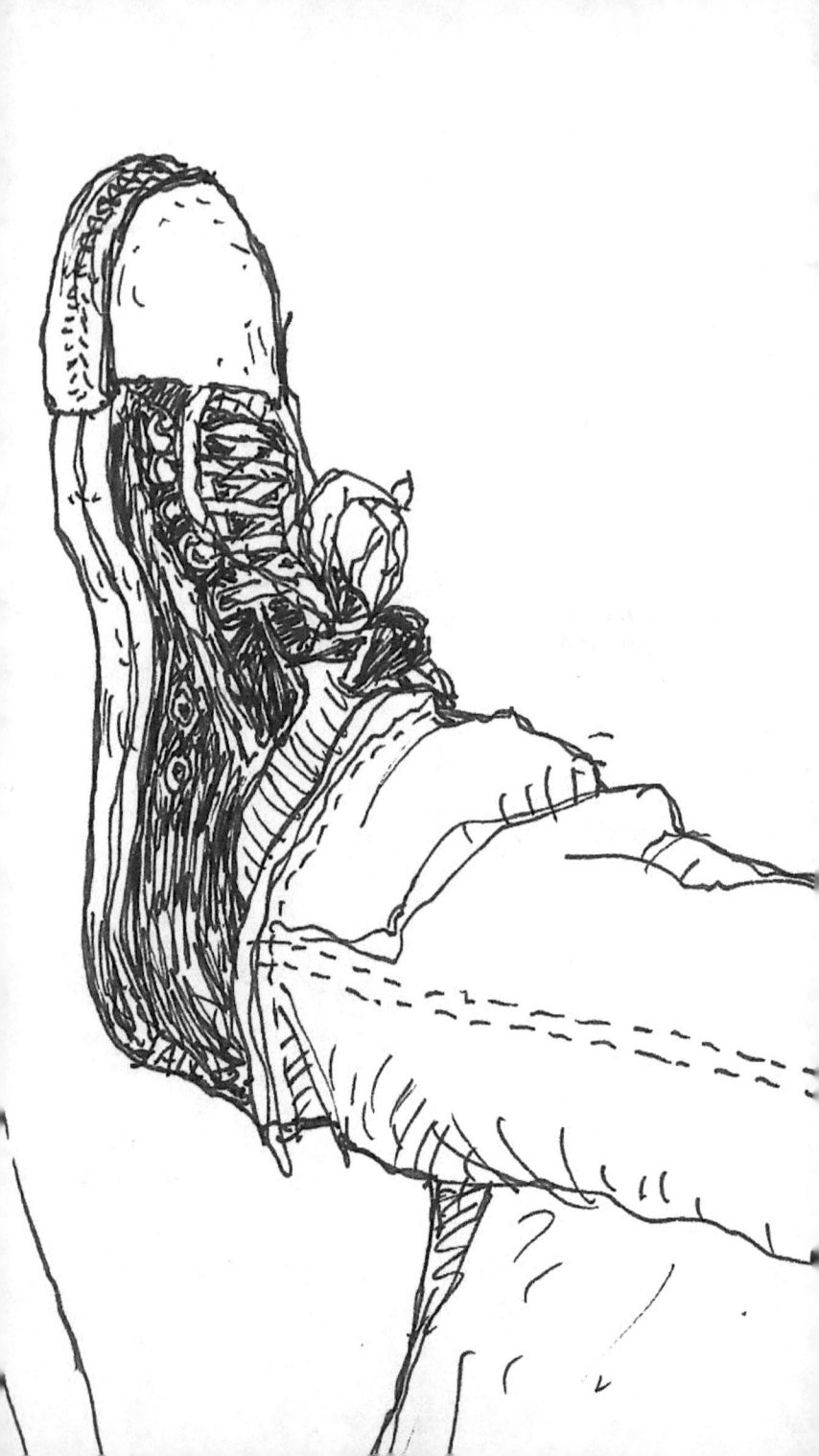

biting an unopened, travel-sized
ALKA-SELTZER pack,
he seems content

if his restless leg unnerves me
— the man in aviators —
more unnerving still:
his shaking leg stops.

like a trappist, he slips his left arm
in his right sleeve, his right
in the left

i tell him that he dropped his glove on the seat
but he believes
i have instructed him
to place his Chihuahua
next to me

reading horatian odes,
he doesn't look up
to catch my yearning

rapping about how
he gonna kill
all dem niggas,
he tastes the feeling
from a polar-bear
COKE can

in backwards cap
studying
a periodic table
he smells like a hoagie

"so, after six hours
you take a shower?"
he confirms
on his smartphone —
then walks
to the next car

it might be rude
to offer my seat
to this old, buff dude

gym shorts and moccasins
with sweater and
jean jacket —
he's a hanging chad

hasidic DON JUAN
for whom even MOSES would break the law

bloodshot eyes in
ADIDAS sweats,
this pothead wants my D

jammed in the seat
by a fat lady
he holds two gloves,
one phone

reading
DEATH IN VENICE,
he's headed down
to battery park

CARHARTT coat and
skintight jeans,
he must be somebody's
pinch-hitter

i always pay
the showtime boys
for commute's
little pleasures

cute show-time boy spreads his legs,
hangs upside-down:
no front teeth

there's a weird bump
like an ear, on his ear,
and his pupils suggest sincerity

since NIKE bought CHUCKS,
their semiotic stock
remains in flux

downcast in a
faded sweatshirt
he's fated not to know
a woman's touch

if not the
designer change purse,
then the heavy mediterranean eyelids
signalize wantonness

i don't care that
this teenage show-time poll-dancer
is only sixteen,
except he hasn't learned to douche

like an art, he practices
the off-the-cuff misanthropy
of an un-offered seat

in olive coat with golden buttons
he unbuttons his shirt
starting to sweat

POLAR EXPRESS cap,
he sits at an angle
turned toward
a newspaper reader
without, however, appearing to know her

cruising this guy,
i didn't notice
for fourteen stops
his wedding ring

sternly scruffy-jowled
with burnished loafers,
he is like an
unworthwhile potato

some white dude
who looks
like my hot cousin SEAN

contra natura are his
haphazard
blowfish smooches

wearing the bleary-eyed hang-over
of frat-dude repression
he tastes the throw-up brewing

like my old pet collie,
his dark eyelashes
look like eyeliner

because the dude
at the end of the car
who is spewing bibimbap
all over the floor
deserves a little privacy,
i will not write
a poem on him

asleep standing up
he licks his lips
dreaming stock options
in the land of lakes

legs askance and torso turned,
arching neck and twisting arm,
feet at angles, texting quick—
he's an easy target for my love

sneering at his FACEBOOK friends,
the DL boy
makes me hard

embroidered rose lining
in his black leather jacket
complicates my view
that his pasty nordic face
connotes RIEFENSTAHL

tight leather pants
and elevated shoes
suggest a pussy pleaser

bobbing his head to invisible music,
he gives me the finger with his eyes

earmuffs and a notebook
probably indicate
a vatic sensitivity

beneath his METS cap
and his RAY CHARLES sunglasses,
all chin

another note-taker
surveys the scene
sucking his pen cap,
a pacifier

this teenage boy
with patchy beard
looks just like TRAYVON

reading his box of prescription toothpaste
the infidel begs
silent forgiveness

chubby buddha
he is at one
but falls asleep
and cracks his phone

as i spy on his crotch
inspecting for gradation
i receive no appreciation
for my ocular blow

men on the platform
(even cuties
who smoke blunts waiting for the C)
are not eligible
for my book

wrapped in a winter scarf
he burns with an innocence
i must destroy

asian man in sunglasses and a racing suit
smells like patchouli

between the crowd
of bundled passengers
he peers at my crotch
with jeepers creepers where you get dem peepers boy

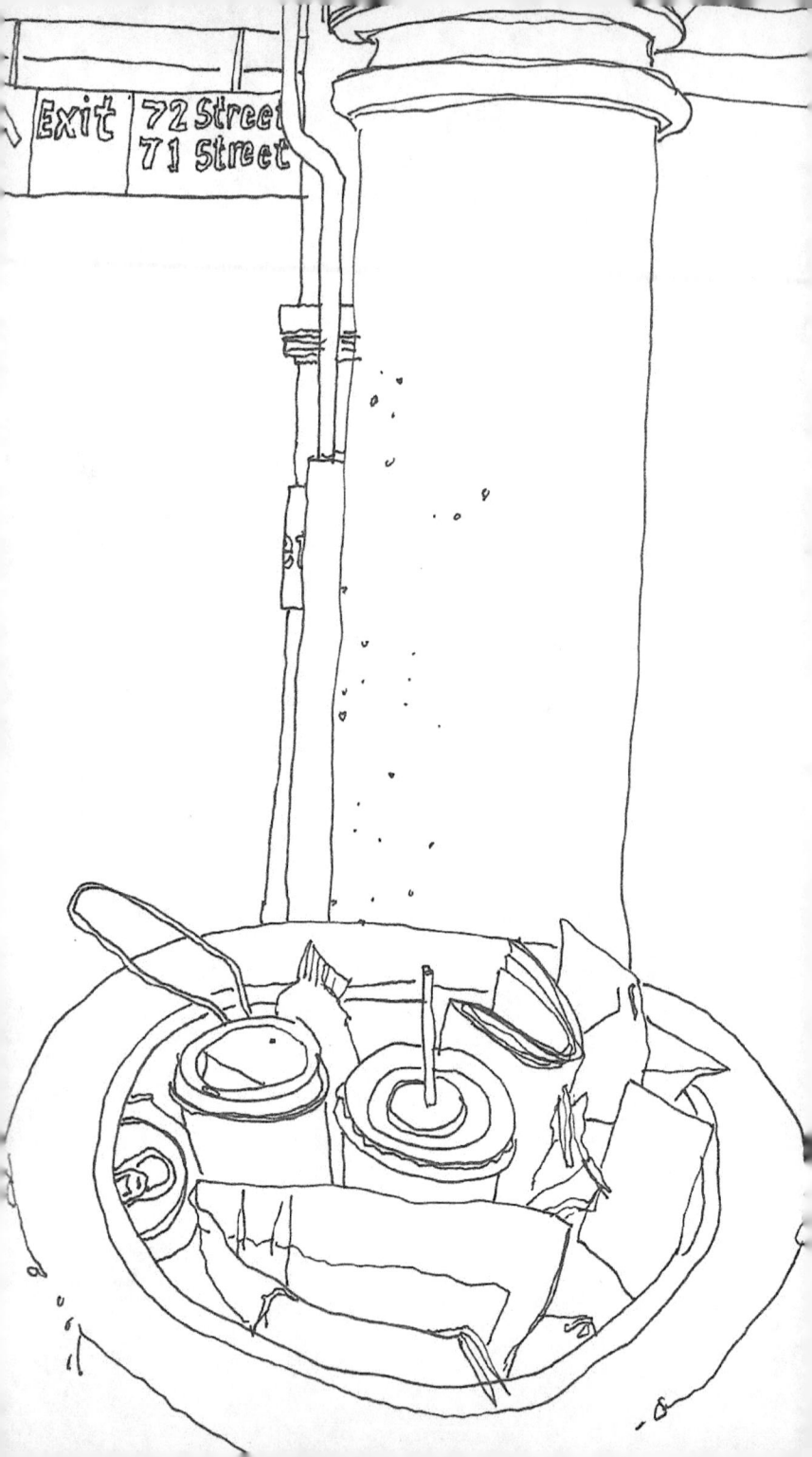

taller and broader than me, the high-yellow boy whose freckles
inspire envy

something about this stranger
suggests to me today
he radically altered his hairstyle —
i gotta switch trains

hair slicked back like
DONALD TRUMP, JR. —
the same,
dick-sucking pout

arab boy decked out
like a dreadlock rasta:
god bless america

short scrawny white boy in giant overcoat,
neanderthal features,
a zen-like indifference

in shorts in december
with gauged ears

what a waste
of fag potential:
the dumpy homo
in pleated pants

scratching his chin, the philosopher
in the YANKEES cap

turned up waxed stache
his perfect posture habituated
to a snarky mommy

jowly, pocky, wrinkly
but cleanly shaven —
the elderly bicycle deliveryman

rugged slavic features
and big fur hat —
no jolly disposition

an apparition in the crowd:
marijuana leaf-print
on drop-crotch sweats

fright-wig hair
and prune face:
a kind of subway hitchhiker

thick neck beard
with faded cheek beard
tilting his head
per aspera ad astra

do-rag projecting
uneasy tenderness

high-lighting every word
of RICHARD II —
an over-eager
joe college

decidedly performing
his disinterest
with blasé baseball cap

peroxide blonde
japanese buzzcut,
inexplicably masculine

another white dude
who looks
like my hot cousin SEAN

straightened hair with
WIFE OF BATH teeth —
definitely a fruit

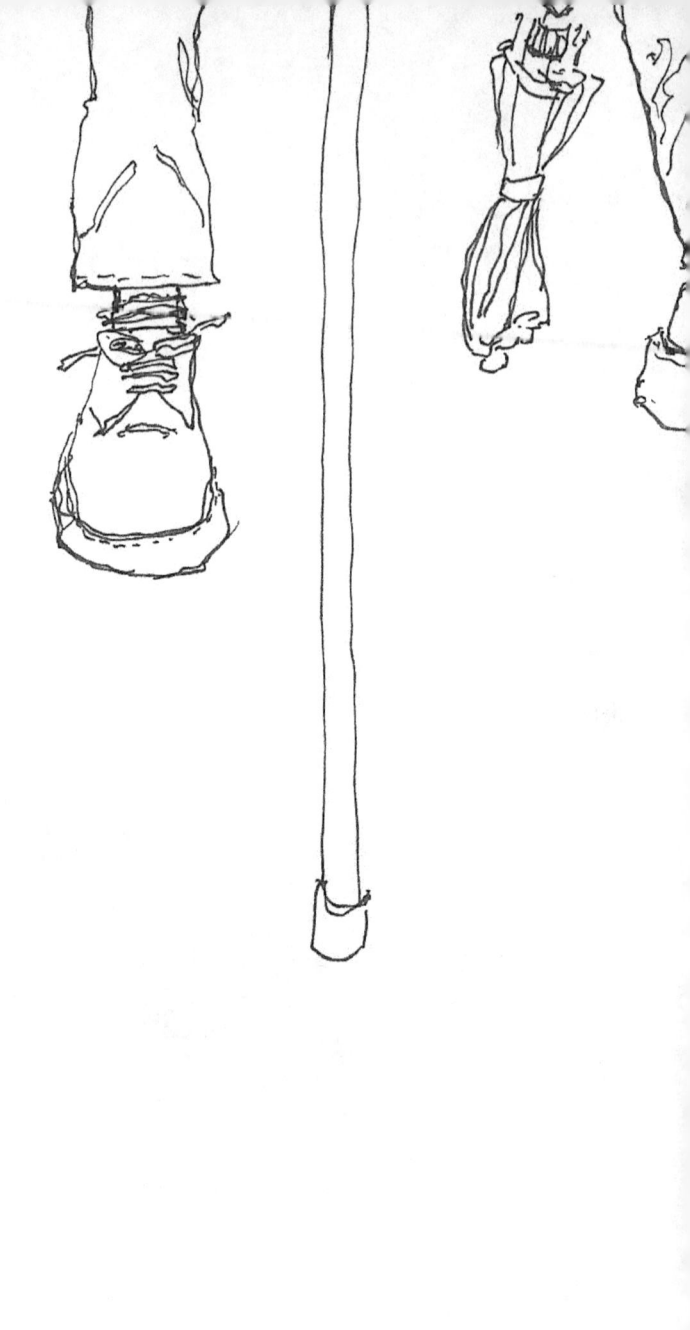

ELDER FOWLER
the mormon missionary
with a taste for espresso

teenage boy
with bowler and
horn-rimmed glasses
studying the cosmos

teenage homo:
greased, thinning hair
and cum on his breath

construction worker with
aquiline nose —
not on the menu

in his front pants pocket
a pack of
MARLBORO REDS,
lightly overbitten lips

pince-nez specs
in defiance of his musculature

NYPD
one-hundred percent
all-american beef—
unlikely candidate
for handcuffing

three hip-hop show-time subway teens
twerking and popping
with no latent homosexual content
whatsoever

mouthing words to his headphones
with eyes rolling along
in J-train ecstasy

showing his ass
giving an angry eyeroll

dread-headed mailman
with wide-spread knees
sipping the MINUTE MAID APPLE JUICE
of midlife regret

leans into his iPhone
with head in hands:
she aint texting back

poncho with highlighter,
college-ruled paper—
playing hard-to-get

some guy in love
with his own reflection —
in the filthy subway window

a middle-aged
straight plumber
on PrEP for the weekend

a dude who looks
like my hot cousin SEAN
in a YALE t-shirt

asian twink with a GUCCI purse —
fat-assed like
nobody's business

old geezer with blinged-out DOPE cap
checking emails

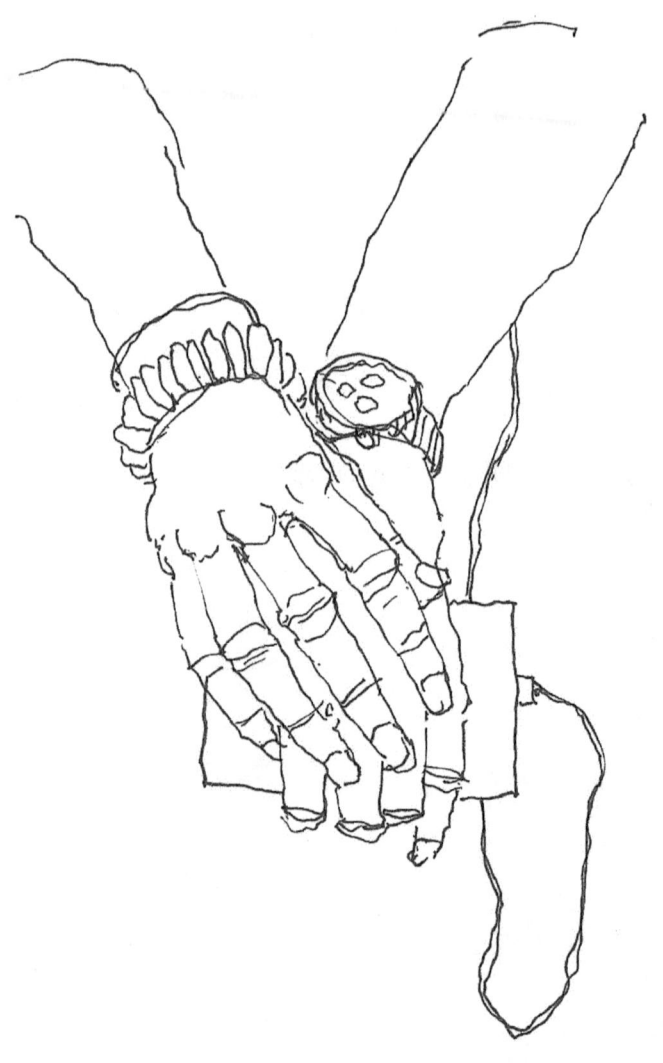

specs on the tip
of his schnoz
spying on neighbors —
the old man
with mud on his thighs

selling WELCH'S FRUIT SNACKS
in aluminum flip-flops,
somehow post-sexual

bad posture like
slouchy gym socks

twelve wicker baskets
stacked in a sack
with his legs folded, prim,
his brow folded,
mad

in Kmart shirt,
freaky-deaky

listening to CHICAGO on his iphone
(the musical, not the band):
the d.l. chubby-chaser

shining bourgeois teeth
skimming GRUNDRISSE

beside his lanky,
buck-toothed sister
with sibling nonchalance:
the towering, lanky, buck-toothed
older brother

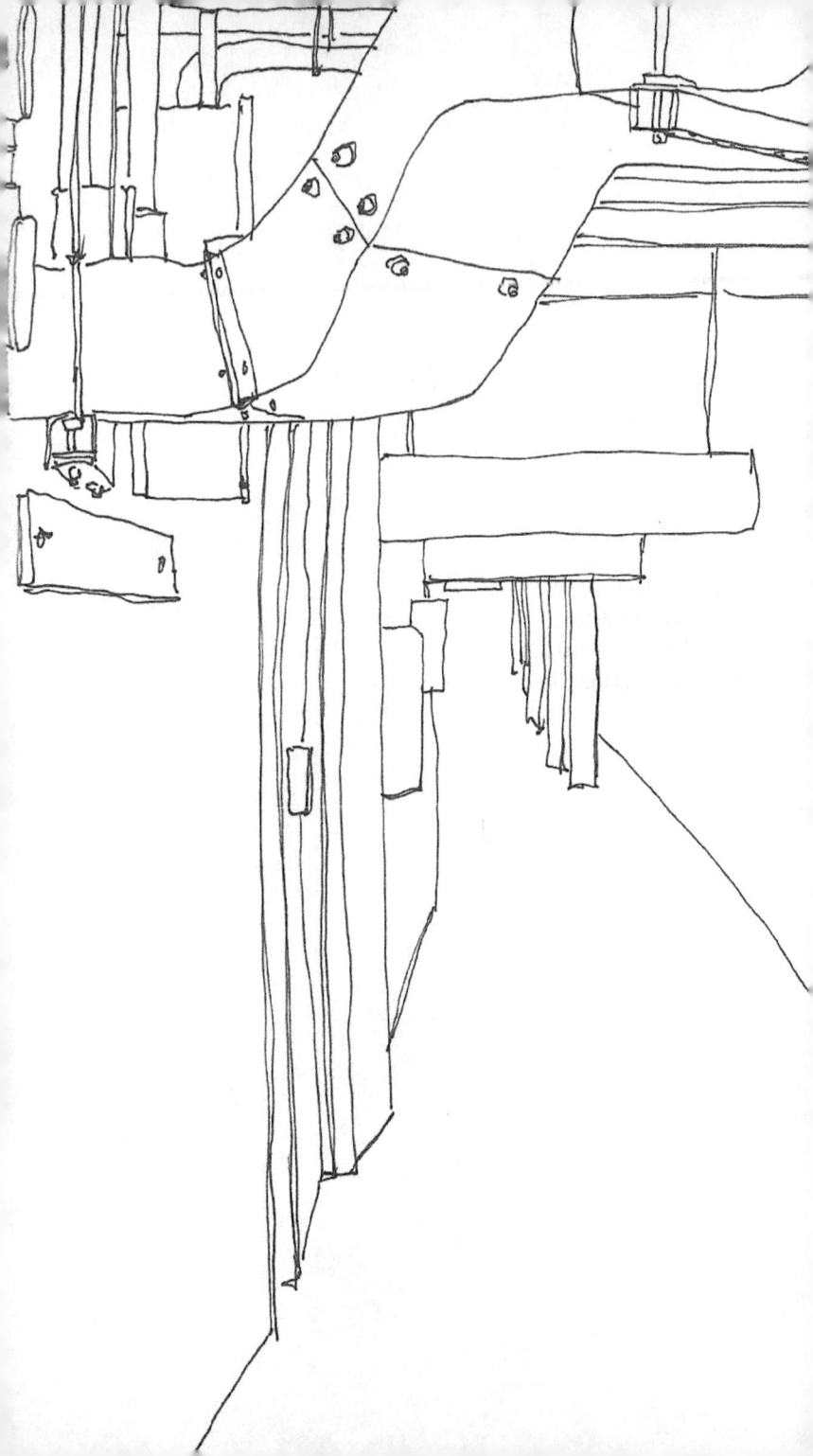

biting the inside of
his cheek,
caressing the outside of his cheek:
an inscrutable case
of itchy cheek syndrome

so much gel in his unstyled hair
nodding at whatever
his straight friend says

impeccably trimmed beard
but rough, ashy skin —
into PnP

thumbs flitting gracefully
playing CRASH BANDICOOT —
IRL, a bad
mamma jamma

twink with a comb-over, desiring
this man's art, that man's ass

narrow eyes and a LITTLE RICHARD stache —
like me, a transfer queen

his uneven stache and lewd gestures:
the decline of the west

his brontosaurus trapezes
credit a deep-throated complacency

his steely squint says
I AINT AFRAID
OF YER DONG
then slaps his hand
on his girlfriend's crotch

his glasses are too large
for a crew cut so short

his pizza delivery backpack
prepares him for a
pizza safari

his eyes linger
on another man's texts
with quiet dignity

his sidelocks long and lush,
his squint overfull
with non-kosher angst

his little leather tote:
a coat of many colors

his pants are rolled up
but his cap pulled down,
indifferent to
libido's call

his restless leg syndrome
in a three-piece suit
is an index of
a hungry hole

his pronounced lean
and pencil-thin eyebrows
suggest impotence

his yellow hat
belongs to his dad
or his daddy

his dour, turned-down lip
and harsh brows
cry out to the lord:
he's a bottom

his lip-ring looks
like a fishhook

his cornrows say
G, but his
chapstick says
mama's boy

his beard is square across the cheek,
semiotically vexed
and quite unattractive

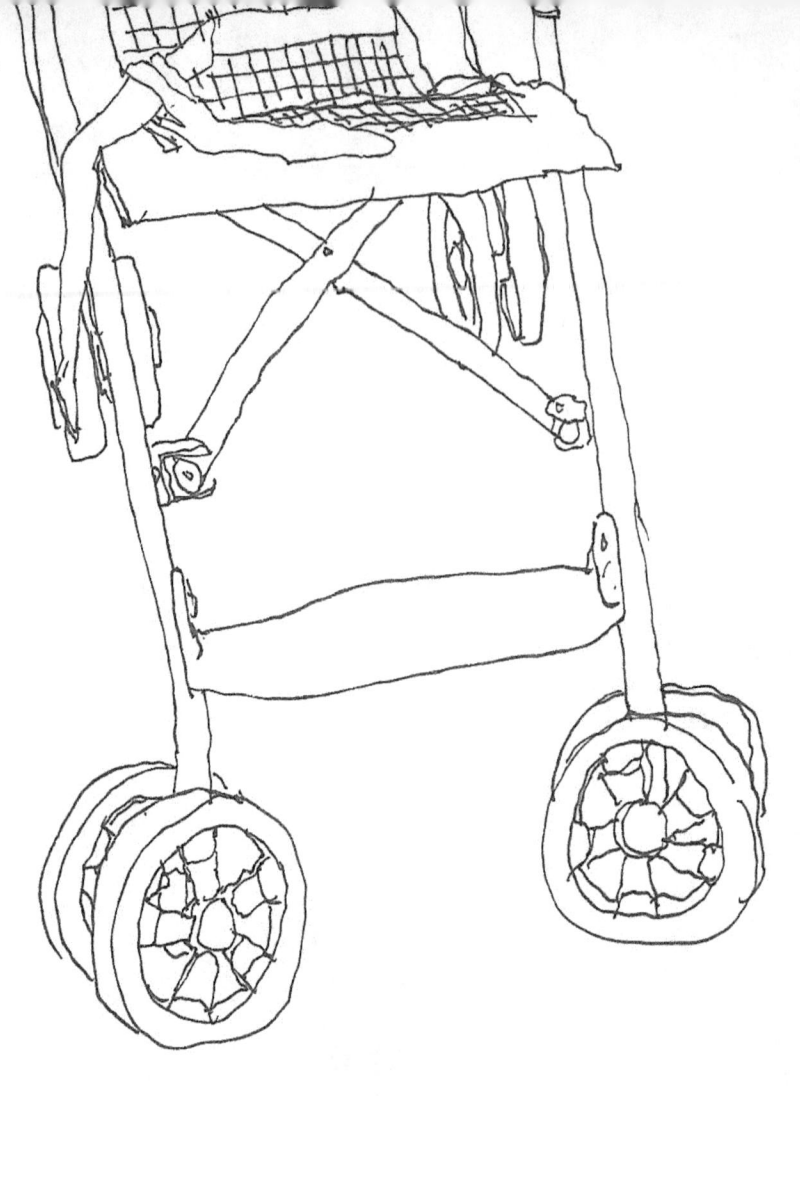

his frizzy hair
and chubby face
make him look tetched:
TELL ME ABOUT THE RABBITS, GEORGE

his bandana divides
his hair and his eyes
like some brechtian mode of alienation
always already recuperated

his canvas bag says
COLUMBIA,
giving the lie
to an histrionic pompadour

his dorky subway sunglasses defy
both function and style
indicating
substance abuse

his bike basket reads
LAW & ORDER SPECIAL VICTIMS UNIT: FILM CREW
THIS VEHICLE IS FOR OFFICIAL THEATRICAL BUSINESS

his head is cocked
like a nervous pheasant
with a lute
between his knees

his shapely clavicle
is below the age
of my muse's consent

his backward golf cap
and quarterback hunch
articulate masochism

his soft chin and the
one strand of bang on his forehead
intimate benevolent patrician

in a COOKIE-MONSTER blue fur coat
and lime green, filthy tennis shoes
he plays
CANDY CRUSH
with pavlovian predictability

a bear with coffee probably wearing
(underneath his
office corduroys)
a studded cockring

a teased-out, space-age afro-puff
on a teenage boy
with tears in his eyes

a chubby cherokee in a BULLWINKLE hat
explains to his fag-hag
the ESTABLISHMENT CLAUSE

a scholar with orange spectacles
mouthing the words
of a JSTOR essay

a CRUSTY with a
carry-out thing
of four STARBUCKS

a high-fashion broach on his lapel
probably means
he's oral-only,
the DORA THE EXPLORER
high-fashion broach
on his boyfriend's lapel:
a sign of codependence

a transparent purse
fat with
newspapers and gluesticks,
fueling my suspicion

a roll of holiday snowflake gift wrap
like a festive phallic scepter,
rereading the
POETRY IN MOTION poster

a green-eyed sissy, diplomatic with
his smartphone

an aristocratic slouch
in shit-kicking heels

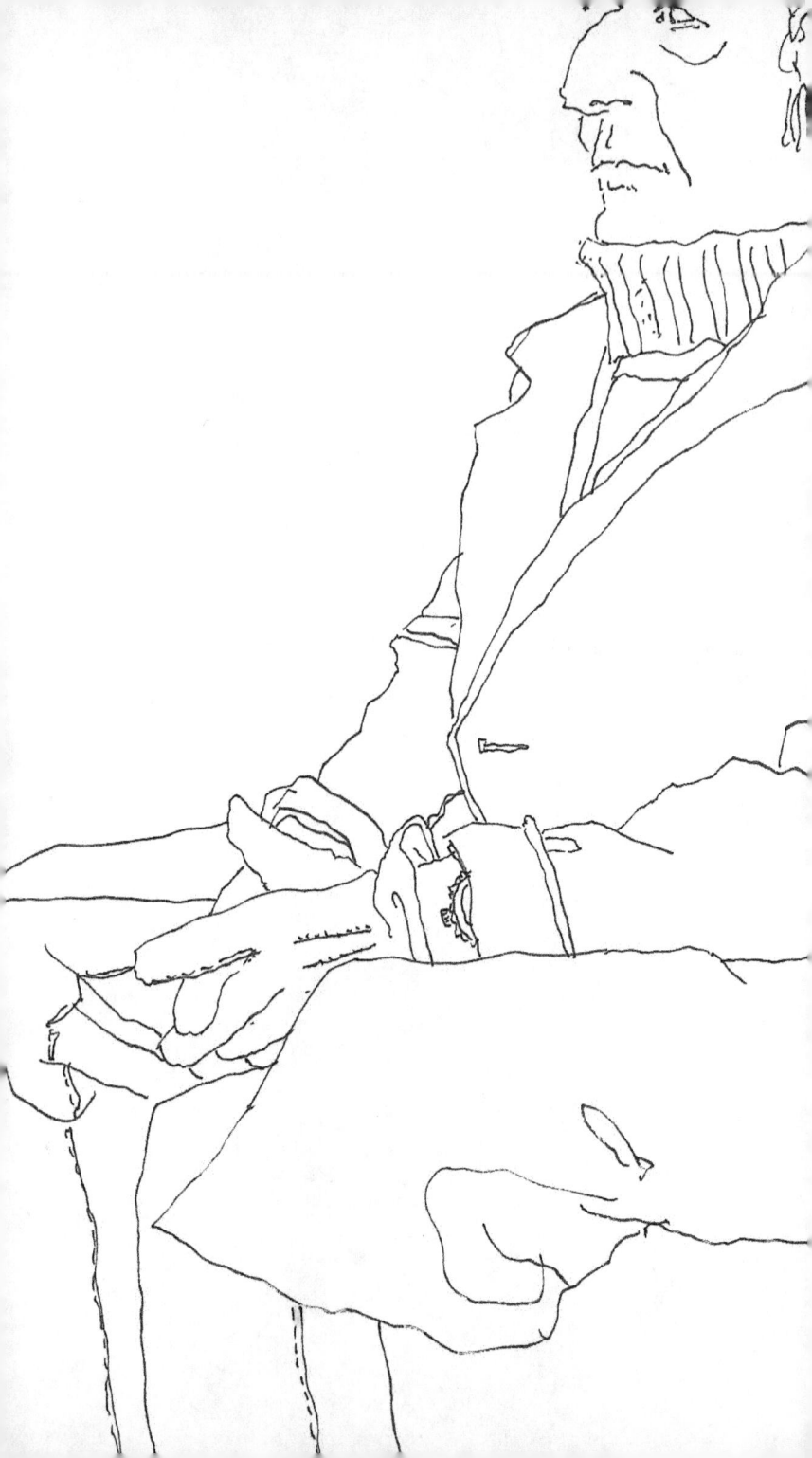

a bright red track-suit
on a teenage brat

a well-fed prole
in a red-knit cap
who probably sports
a chode

a hollow-cheeked black
with over-packed suitcase—
not bound
for LAGUARDIA

an angel-headed hipster
destroyed by madness and
OLD NAVY PERFORMANCE FLEECE

a mohawked CRUSTY in a neckbrace laying on
the floor yelling:
it only takes 5 people
10 cents each
to give a junkie
50 cents

a scowling black nationalist who likes
white dudes
who rim him

a varsity letter jacket
growing up to be
a debaser

a jerry-curled boy
asleep in a shawl
like baby JESUS

a pensive
DIESEL shopper
heading to the next car
makes a timely BREXIT

an unattended youth
with LISA FRANK binder
sends mixed signals

a PANTHER beret and a pleated skirt:
either a commie or faggot or both

a scruffy bookworm
caught in a simple misunderstanding
with his polka-dot loafers

the homeless man
exposing himself
performs a public service

the man in paisley
pursues the NEW YORK TIMES CROSSWORD
with a purple gel pen

the dark-skinned fellow
with HARPO MARX peroxide puff
kindly offers his seat

the sidelocks of this hasidic bucher:
NELLIE OLESON,
arch-rival of
LITTLE HOUSE

the guy who cruised me
(sashaying up and
down the platform)
now sits across
and won't deign flirt

the pakistani kid
with prematurely salt-
and-pepper hair
belongs in my
superpac commercial

the dude in the hoodie
smiles as he catches me
writing my christmas list

the old man, angry,
dissertates aloud
about blue lipstick

the cartoon bumble-bee on his hat
persuades me of his humanity

the shrunken-face teen
is giving me the willies
as he commits
a misdemeanor

the gaping-mouth twinky arab boy
with his two hirsute buddies
pats his friend's thigh, intoning
"habibi, habibi"

the tattoo on his left hand may say
MONEY TICKLES
(but ink is hard to read on skin so dark)

the clean-cut, well-dressed catamite
removes his gloves revealing his
prison-tat
knuckles

the pink-haired pixie boy
kicks a stranger's bag
just for the hell of it

the frayed denim
around the hole
in his jeans at the knee
he twists coquettishly

the YANKEES fan who picks his nose
while wearing one glove
potentially barebacks

the bro with bangs
poking out of his hat
regrettably must explain to his girlfriend
they missed their stop

the pasty homo
a MODIGLIANI
in an H&M suit

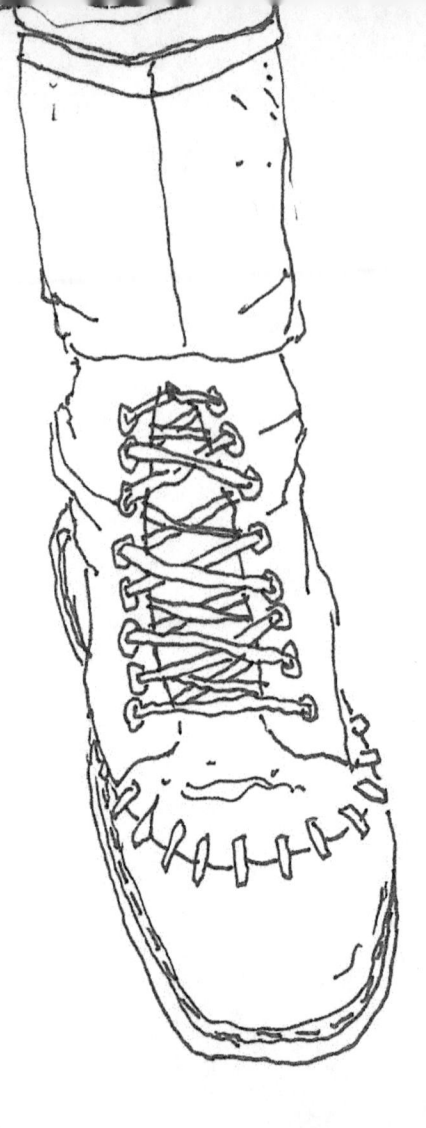

the misfolded brim
paradoxically shows
joie de vivre

the homeless, rail-thin white dude
with a grocery bag of
his own vomit
works for the CIA

the teenage wunderkind with a top-knot
looks at me angrily
like i just grounded him

the name tattooed around his throat is
(from this distance)
not quite legible, but
i stare too long and he approaches
with murder in his eyes

the triangular cut
on his nose
in the shape of a
cartoon nose

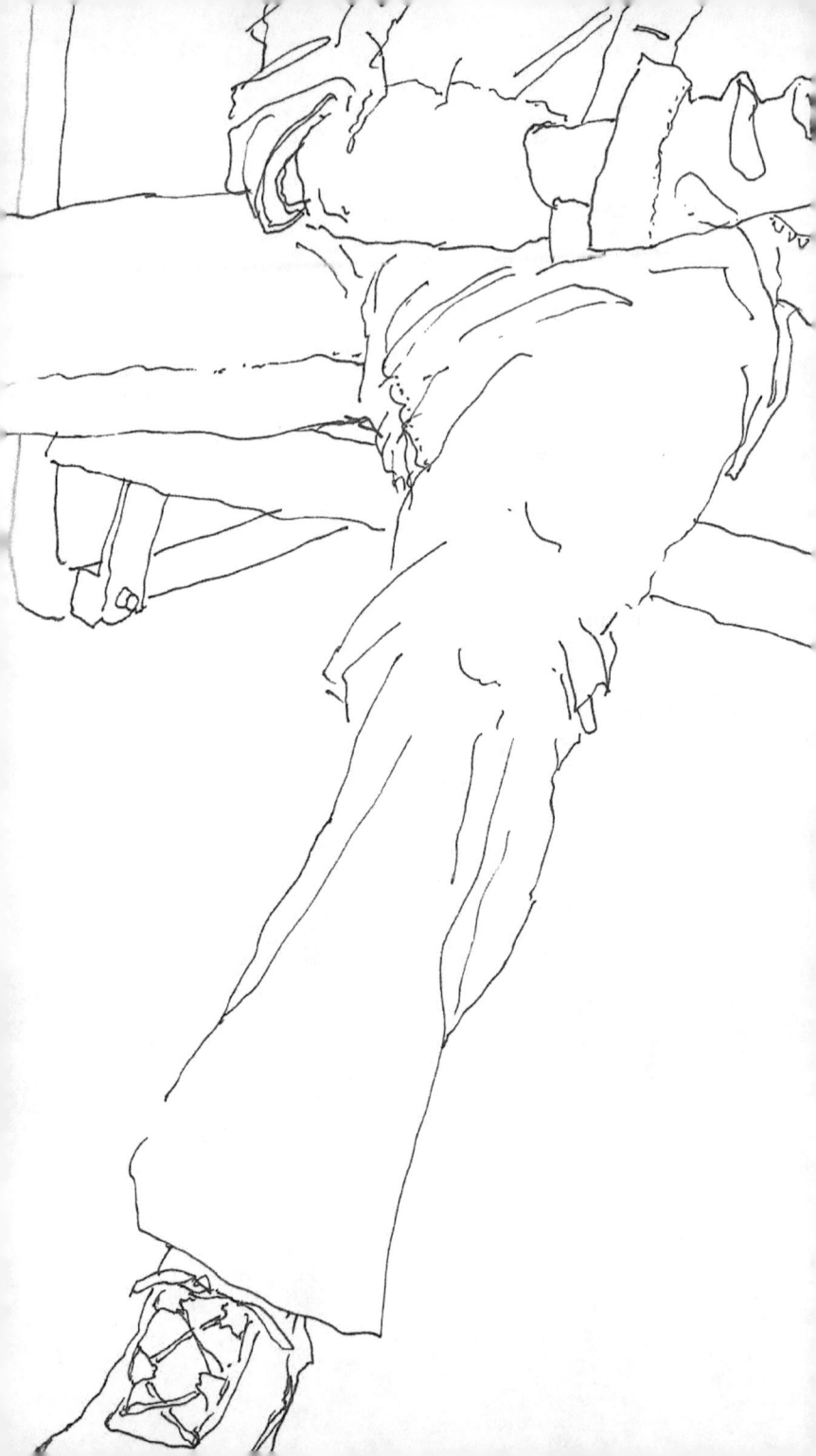

the bear with a crease on his nose bridge
& stack of
unopened mail:
his baseball cap says SORRY MOM

the busking drummer tells us to have
a blessed day
but there's no guarantee

the trim on his strap
like an ancient phoenician trading ship
hunkered down
for some sexting

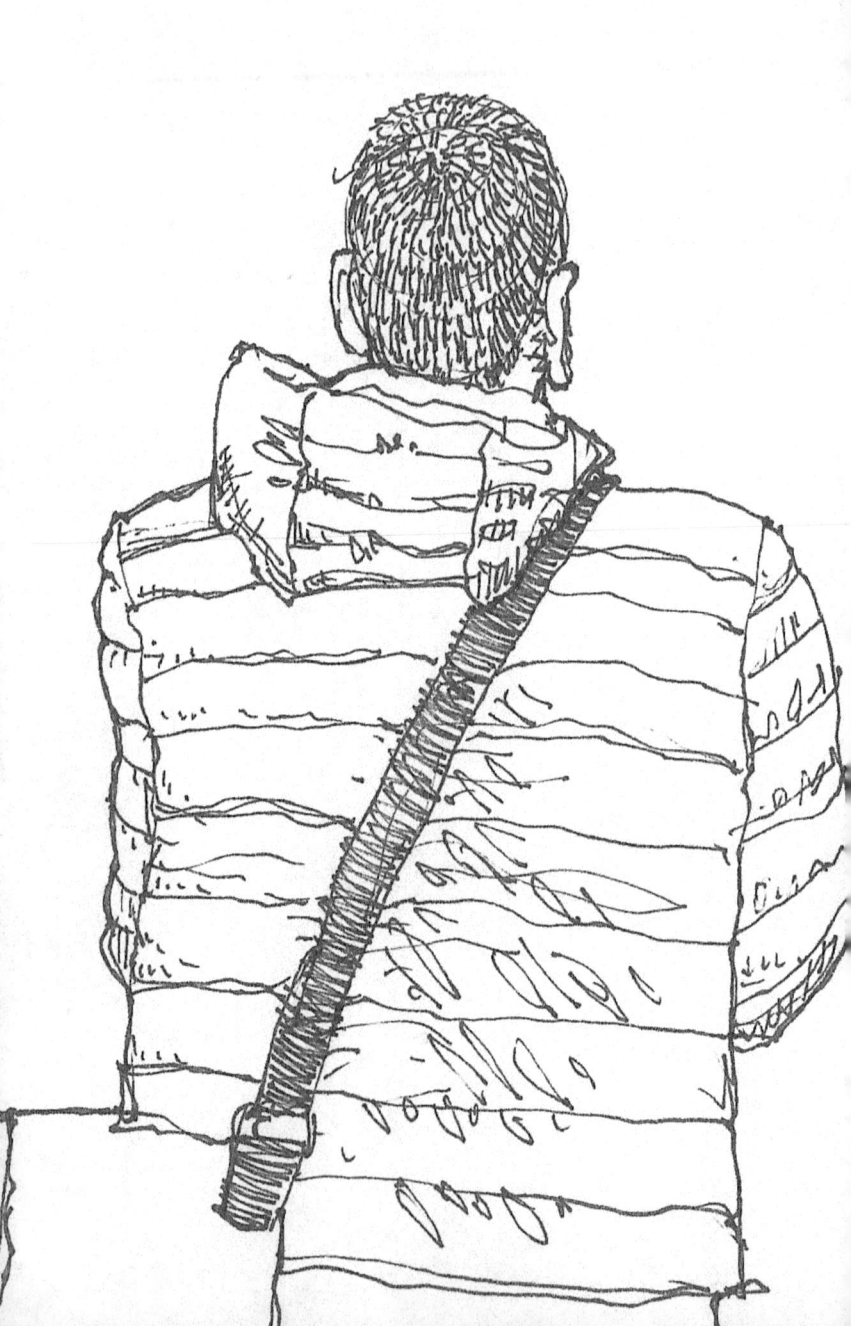

the rough-red stigmatism on his left eye
takes the derivative
of mid-life crisis
over teenie-bopper
cut-off tee

the camus nose of a pakistani businessman
recalls the REEVE'S TALE

the CRUSTY with a
heart of gold
has a worried mom
back ST. LOUIS

the long silver chain dangling
from one back pocket to
the other back pocket
is a butt necklace

the undershirt beneath his collared shirt
cuts his neckline, revealing
the calloused glans of circumcised straightness

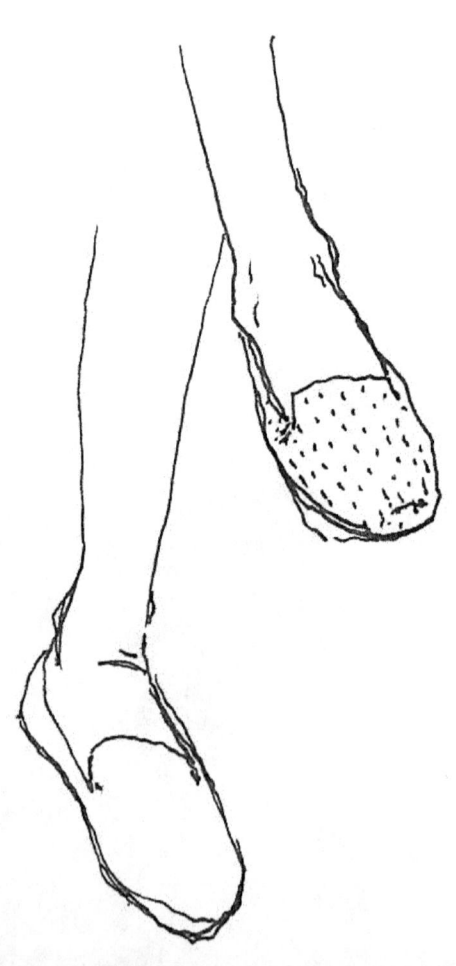

the contrapposto of this
CANDY-CRUSHER is
polymorphously perverted

the accordion panels
in his drop-crotch jeans
are mama's little squeeze box

the rip in his pants —
a window to his soul

the flesh rolls on his upper leg
tightly bound in khakis
appear to me
like a pussy

the strange flatness of his nose
offsets and recomposes
his lack of a chin
until he is seen as
classically beautiful
like the marble bust
of some demonic
child emperor

he stuffs one napkin into his mother's coat pocket
then blows a snot-load into his other napkin

he smiles wryly as he texts a friend:
"i'm dumping her ass"

he carries his earbuds in his teeth
having swallowed the red pill

he drinks from a paper coffee cup
branded UFT
forlorn pedagogue
of unending whiteboards

he's got that lone-gunman look
as he caresses the back of the knee
of some little wifey who's charged with
re-directing
his demons

he frowns determinedly
composing a manifesto,
a ski-mask framing
his wine-dark lips

he twists his lips, perplexed,
but his eyes in
placid focus
beam inner peace

he kind of squats
to zip his fly
with a pleased smile

he taps his phone
exactly how
i'd tap his butt

he tells his interlocutor
that they must part ways
at GRANDMA AVENUE

he wears a lime and gray flannel shirt
like the one I wore
in a former life

he looks like my student, AWN,
(the hot pakistani chemistry major)
but less hot than AWN
because
he hasn't shaved
his patchy beard

he presses his leg against mine,
the horny teen playing MARIO CART,
pwning some noobs

he has a very small face
and (with his hands in his pockets)
disappears

he keeps taking photos of himself,
the nondescript guy
whose carpenter's pencil
tells the whole story

he pursues the subway like personals ads,
his expansive
song-of-self

he wears cargo pants
without any cargo

he is a J CREW editorial
well-built and
expertly tailored
but biting his thumb nail

he wears the sunglasses and dreads
of a vietnam vet

he has his hands
clasped behind his back
like some french
cabinet minister

he wears a paint-splattered track suit
as he reattaches
a saint's medallion

he's 42 but still admires
HOLDEN CAULFIELD

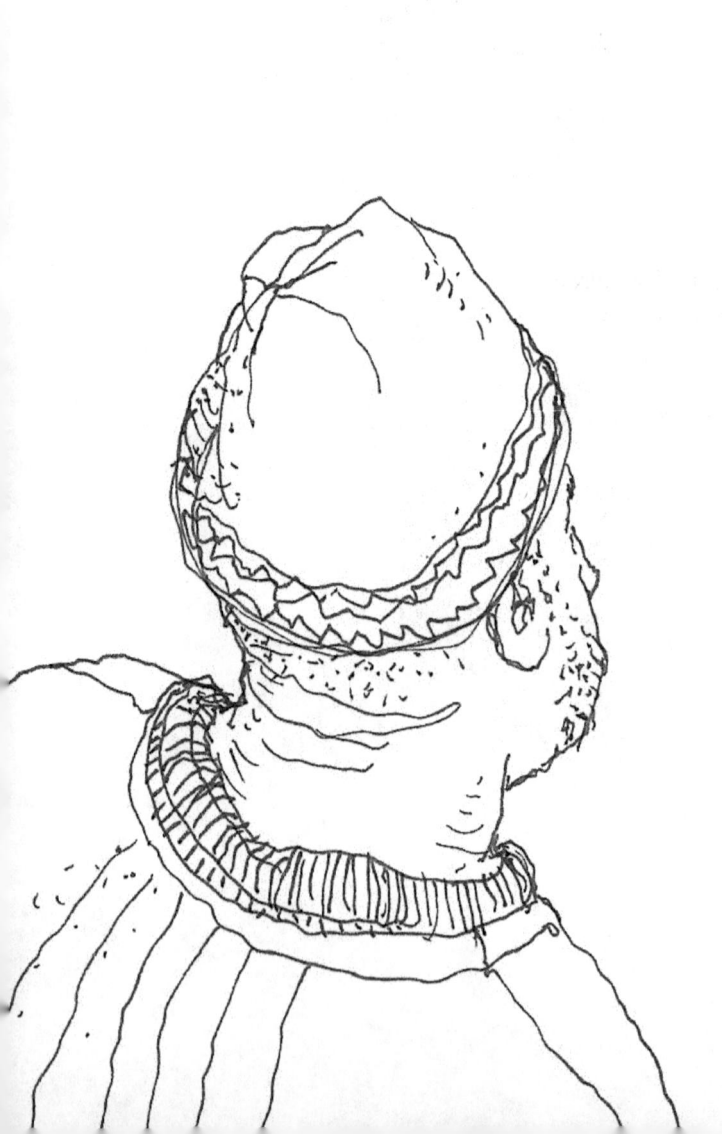

he twirls his pointer to
an earbud song
with sinister intent

he is decked out in
vestiges of
feudal finery

he watches
a *parodia* vid
on YOUTUBE
with spanish subtitles
i can barely translate

he looks exactly like my ex-boyfriend
(the one who got his eye beat out by a
homeless man)
but it's not him

(DREW has to wear
an eyepatch now)

he glares at me, then dims his eyes—
an enigma

he holds his
adam's apple
with thumb and forefinger
like an apotropaic talisman
to ward off castration

he talks loudly
about his ex-girlfriend's suicide
but i'm a sucker
for man-splainers

he has his priorities
in order, scarfing
kung-pow chicken

he has a rosebush sleeve tat
up his thick olive bicep:
poor banished children of EVE

he touches my leg
with GRINDR open on his cellphone
and gives me his number
but has blue gums

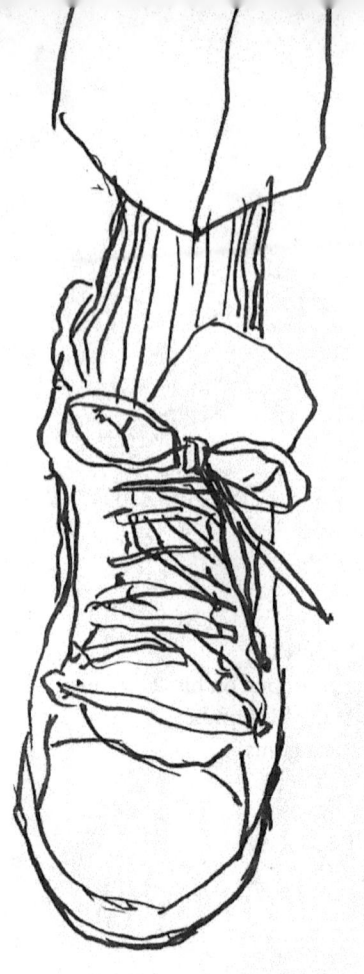

he has the same
faux-leather
bag as me,
but i'm gayer

he will be unable
to explain his MARSHALLS splurge
to penny-pinching wife

he rests his umbrella against his unzipped fly
gazing without hope

he wears baby-blue UGGS
with a SPONGEBOB bookbag
and a construction worker's helmet —
my scanning inconclusive

he has evidently caught the transfer
from the F to the M
at west fourth street

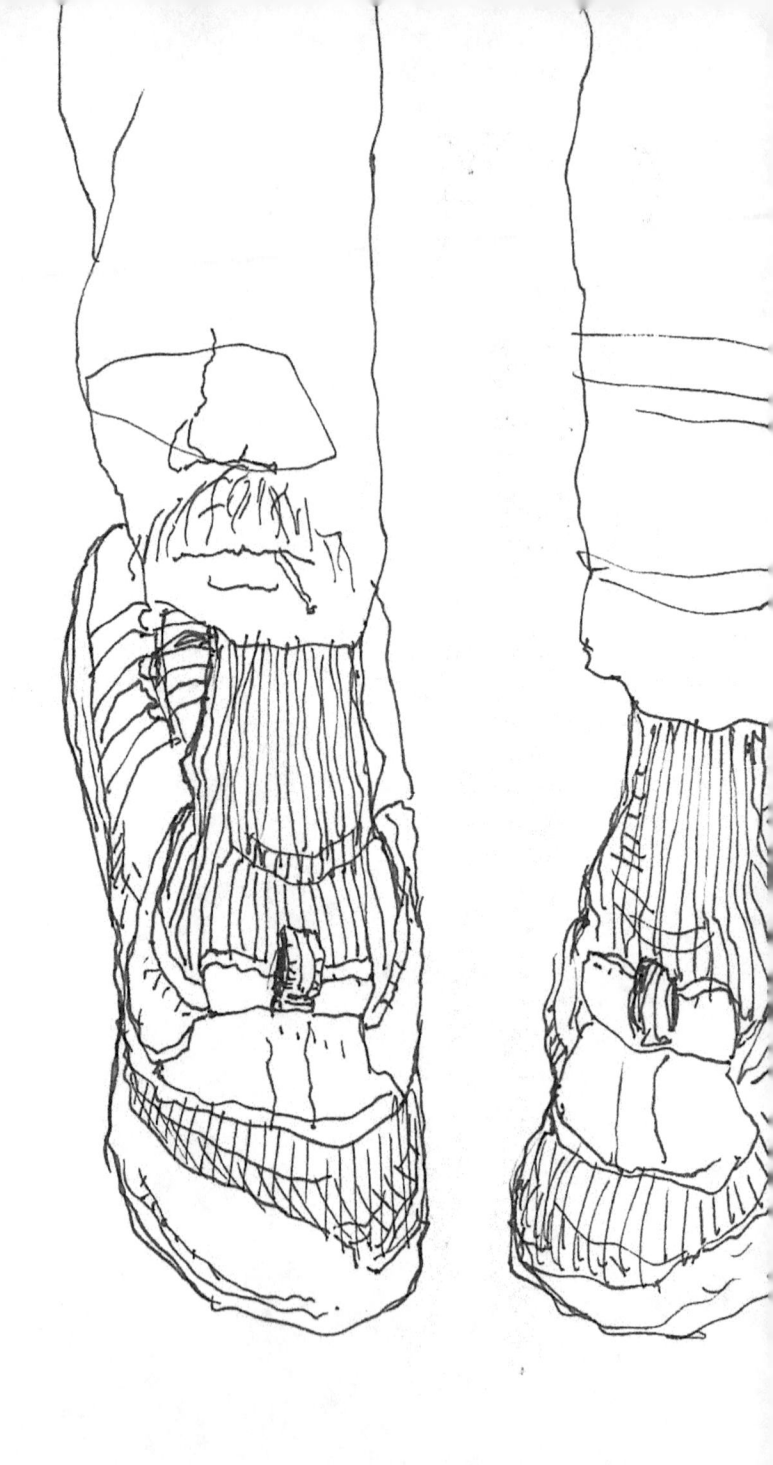

he trimmed his
neck-beard
upon some YOUTUBE style vid advice

are those big buggy eyes the product
of coke-bottle lenses
or a CHENEY-esque exit strategy?

does this pre-pubescent boy need
a permission slip
to wax those eyebrows so fiercely?

in capris, he carries a cherry wood
folding table
a christmas gift from nana, or for her?

what is
THRASHER MAGAZINE and why is he
wearing their hat—
this black hipster with white girl—
a peer-reviewed journal on jungle fever?

why do mexican bus boys only ever
grow to 5 feet 4,
i silently ask
this teeny hottie?

how can someone so tall
plead so for love?

is this very tall old man
squeezed between
two girls
committing predation?

how does the
doe-eyed traveler
staring at my forehead
avoid my eyes
these many stops
to BUSHWICK?

why does this man stare at my shoes
griping a
POLAND SPRING?

tortoise-shell glasses and a LAKERS hat —
something tells me he's celibate:
maybe his ecstatic stare?

long curly hair
like a renaissance courtier —
perhaps he's texting
machiavellian schemes?

a palestinian
solidarity scarf
on a chubby jew —
but is he a fruit?

guy with
bloody chapped lips,
why do you mutter conspiratorially
about DEREK JETER?

his cheeks, hollowed by pock-marks
lend a simian flair —
but do apes get zits?

chinese boyfriend speaks to his
chinese girlfriend
with squeaky chinese accent —
why not speak chinese?

help me disambiguate
the holes in his jeans:
is he slutty or
grungy or both?

is that businessman lost in a heroin slouch?
no, he just can't get his zipper unstuck

long-haired chubby guy in green hoodie and green trousers —
from MIDDLE EARTH?

in hounds-tooth trousers,
a package-bulge or camel-toe?

the asian boy with muttonchops
throws me off —
can't tell if he's gay or
even if
right now
i am?

he holds his fist
on his heart, beating to
what earbud song?

he puts his hand
on her thigh
like it's his own thigh
— maybe it somehow is?

a grumpy skater boy
with poor-little-rich-girl eyes —
or is it
BETTE DAVIS eyes?

MALCOLM X look-alike
he is half-asleep
like getting picked up from grandmas

some fat
KEVIN SPACEY with
a flannel hunting hat —
solving the race crisis

he looks like
CLARK GABLE with a
runny nose from poppers

he smells like
a roachbutt
thugged out and asleep
somehow recalling
PAUL SIMON

LEE HARVEY OSWALD pudgy
playing CANDY CRUSH

MARILYN MONROE beauty mark
on his left cheek
which i would smear with cum but which probably
interferes with his shaving

little cutie pie
with REAGAN hair
didn't cover when coughing
and needs to get spanked

JABBA THE HUT face
but a PRINCESS LEIA torso
wrapped in a sheet

slicked hair
like RALPH FIENNES in SCHINDLER'S LIST
with similar bad-boy appeal

grasping the pole and
leaning back like
my own TYLER DURDEN

giving me side-eye
he's reading the gospel according to
SAINT MATT

hands crossed over his belt buckle,
an unlikely gesture of reverence
given his SCARFACE teeshirt

like BORIS KARLOFF
giving me the once over,
has a frankenstein dick

in airbrushed camouflaged sweats
he smells like popcorn
and looks like PUTIN

long silver hair and big horse teeth
this dude is as horny
as EILEEN MYLES

WILLEM DEFOE face
checking his hair in
his phone

this stank-face twink
is just begging
to get sero-converted

this straight dude
wears a sour, faggy frown
because his girl
just chewed him out

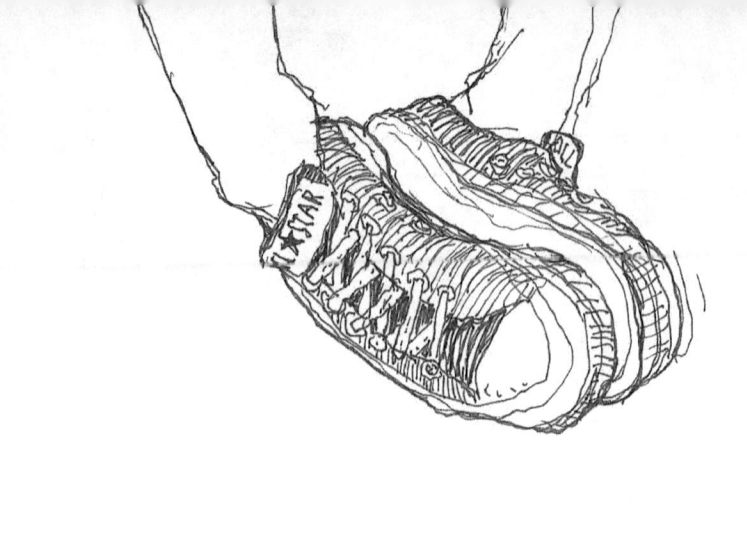

this faded, flat-topped hustler,
whose weary eyes
graze my bulge

this NEW YORK TIMES devotee
has a crush on
PAUL KRUGMAN

this pretty boy
in UNDER ARMOUR
makes my day

the homeless man beside his
trash bag kingdom
reads a xeroxed essay from FORBES

old man folded in a death pose
like PICASSO's blue guitarist
— i yearn to be so detached:
but did he just wink?

with a blue scarf, blue hat, and blue book
the lonely reader doesn't notice me.

also, blue tennis shoes.

polka-dot shoes
(blue with pink spots)
he cock-blocks me
with a game of
CANDY CRUSH

DORITO dust
on his blue suede shoes
strangely apropos

blue contacts make
his brown eyes gleam,
no homo

what the young novelist
types into
his smartphone:

"what the hell is that?" daywalker yelled.
"it's really happening," ricky replied.

another LITTLE RICHARD stache

unpolished loafers,
a slow sort of suicide

appearing before
in this book
(in a coat like
COOKIE MONSTER):
today he wears
a dreary flak jacket

falling asleep
with an eyeball
painted on his eyelid
warding off naughty spirits

DION, in a SHAKE-SHACK uniform, explains he's not
a bum but his mom has
stage-four cancer

receding hairline
like a ruined
greek amphitheater
and a face like my hot cousin SEAN

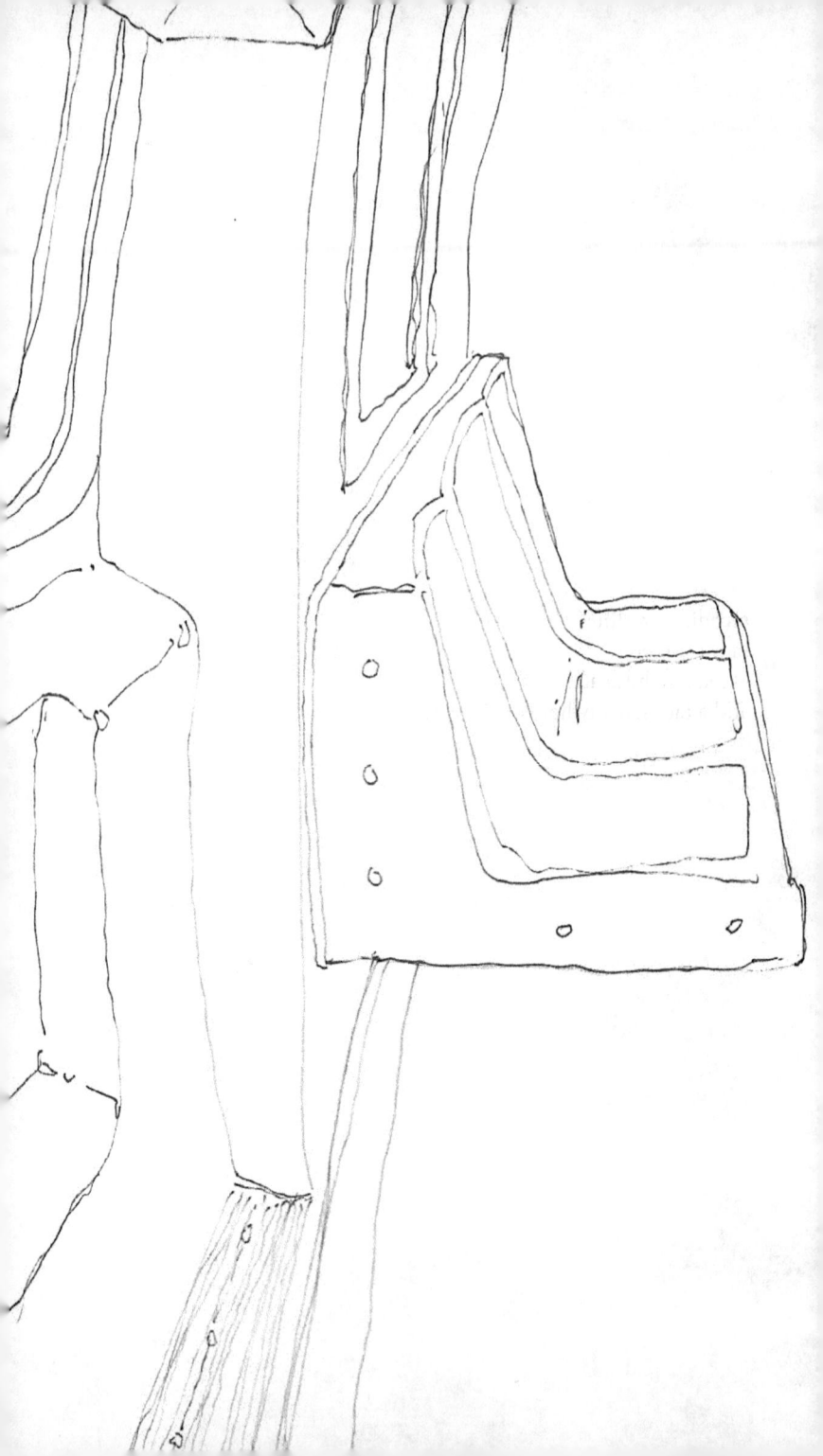

O, emerald-eyed BORICUA,
you inspire my
politically-incorrect
fear of
demonic possession!

O, JASON, selling your WELCH'S FRUIT SNACKS:
let me vouch for you
at the parent/teacher conference!

O, baller in JACKIE O glasses,
you carry CHARMIN, proclaiming
no femmes no fats no asians!

O, short papi chulo,
can't tell if you're gay
or if you're illegal!

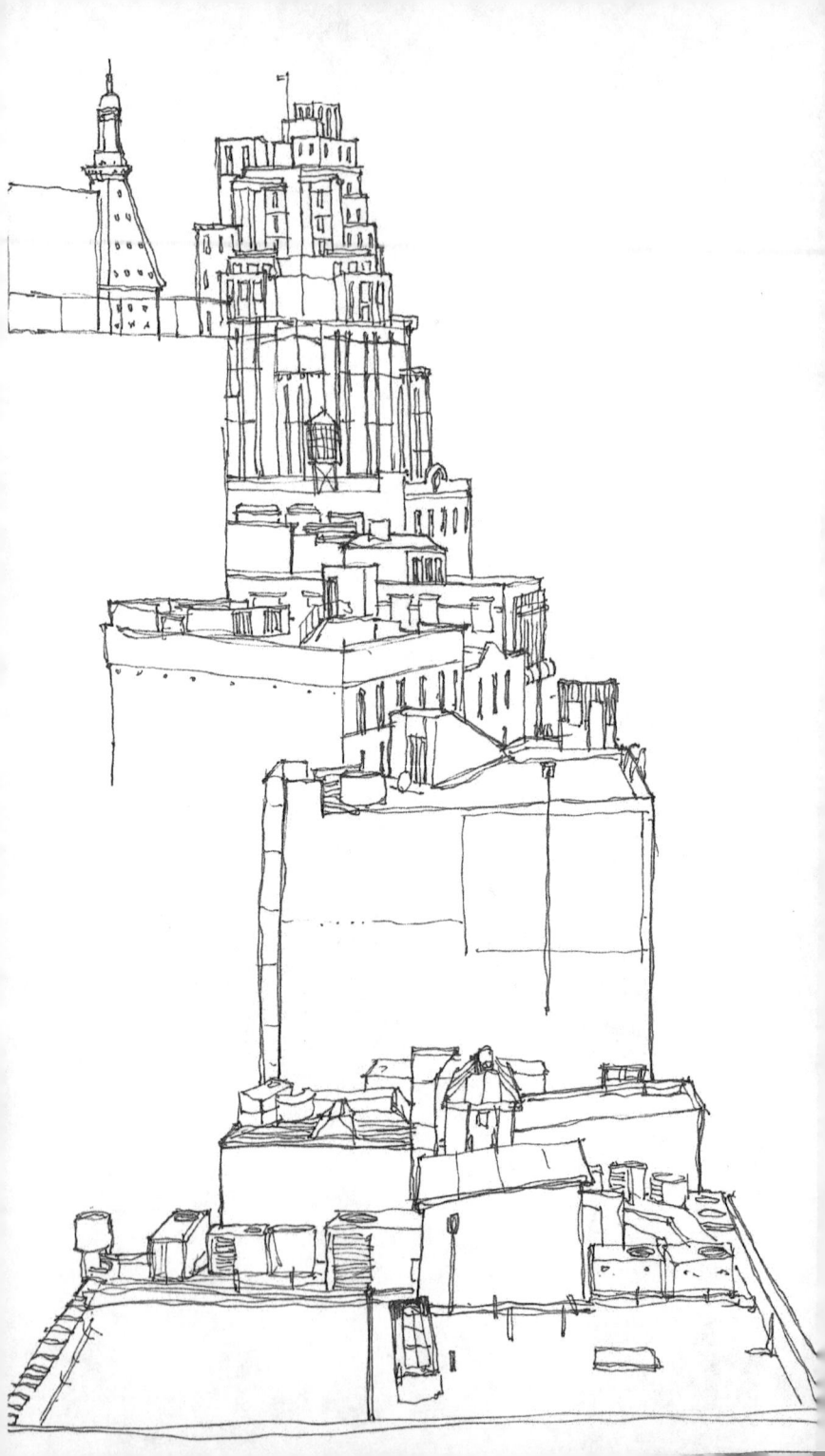

A.W. is a poet who lives in Brooklyn and teaches medieval literature at CUNY. Strouse is also the other of My Gay Middle Ages *(punctum books, 2015).*

Patty grew up in Utah, was schooled in Ohio, and lives in Brooklyn, where he runs a custom fabrication studio.

www.ingramcontent.com/pod-product-compliance
Lightning Source LLC
Chambersburg PA
CBHW071734150426
43191CB00010B/1567